P9-DGL-918

Classic
VEGETARIAN

Classic VEGETARIAN

Appetizing dishes for every occasion

FOREWORD BY
SARAH BROWN

SMITHMARK

© 1996 Anness Publishing Limited

This edition published in 1996 by
SMITHMARK Publishers, a division of US Media Holdings, Inc
16 East 32nd Street
New York NY 10016
USA

SMITHMARK books are available for bulk purchase for sales promotion and for premium use. For details write or call
the Manager of Special Sales, SMITHMARK Publishers, 16 East 32nd Street, New York, NY 10016; (212) 532–6600.

Produced by Anness Publishing Limited
1 Boundary Row
London SE1 8HP

All rights reserved. No part of this publication may be reproduced,
stored in a retrieval system, or transmitted in any way or by any means,
electronic, mechanical, photocopying, recording or otherwise,
without the prior written permission of the copyright holder.

ISBN 0-8317-7382-0

Publisher Joanna Lorenz
Senior Cookery Editor Linda Fraser
Cookery Editor Anne Hildyard
Designer Nigel Partridge
Illustrations Madeleine David
Photographers Karl Adamson, Steve Baxter, James Duncan and Michael Michaels
Recipes Alex Barker, Roz Denny, Christine France, Annie Nichols and Steven Wheeler
Food for photography Carole Handslip, Wendy Lee and Jane Stevenson
Stylists Madeleine Brehaut, Hilary Guy, Blake Minton and Kirsty Rawlings
Jacket photography Amanda Heywood

Typeset by MC Typeset Ltd, Rochester, Kent
Printed and bound in China

Picture on frontispiece: Horizon International Images

CONTENTS

Foreword 6

Introduction 8

Starters 10

Main Courses 16

Pasta, Rice, and Pizzas 40

Desserts 56

Index 64

FOREWORD

I became a vegetarian about 20 years ago when I was running a wholefood shop. From the very beginning I experimented with the ingredients I stocked, creating recipes and eventually selling food in my shop. So many people liked the results that I soon opened a restaurant, later sharing my recipes with an even wider public when I became a cookery writer. At that time vegetarian food hardly qualified as a cuisine. Many people viewed a vegetarian meal as something that consisted of a few vegetables and a space on the plate where the meat should have been!

During the last decade or so, vegetarian food has really come into its own. It is now seen as a cuisine in its own right, as this lovely book of classic recipes shows.

I have always drawn on ideas from all around the world to create interesting recipes, so I am pleased that Classic *Vegetarian* does exactly that. You can travel to Thailand and Italy and the Middle East without ever leaving your kitchen. Fresh herbs and exotic seasonings add an authentic note to many of the dishes.

The versatility of vegetarian food is amply illustrated by recipes for every occasion, from nutritious family meals to sophisticated suggestions for celebrations. If you are new to vegetarian cooking, look out for the useful Cook's Tips, which help you save time, offer hints on preparation or suggest different ways of adapting the recipe to suit your own requirements.

For anyone who is still worried about how to fill that space on the plate, this book provides plenty of food for thought. It is packed with good classic recipes which use a wide variety of healthy ingredients to produce dishes that are full of flavor, easy to make, and based on sound nutritional principles.

SARAH BROWN

INTRODUCTION

This book celebrates the variety, versatility, and sheer enjoyment offered by a vegetarian diet. The old image of meat-free meals as dull but worthy has long since disintegrated, and today's vegetarian meals are fresh, light, and appetizing. Nor do you have to be a practicing vegetarian to enjoy them: the increasing emphasis on healthy eating means that more and more families sit down several times a week to a meal of pasta or rice with vegetables or a cheese sauce, and the fact that meat does not feature is incidental rather than intentional. Few restaurant menus fail to feature a vegetarian dish, and whereas this was once invariably some sort of vegetable lasagne, the trend now is to offer more exciting and innovative dishes. Green Lentils with Sweet Onions and Broccoli and Chestnut Terrine feature in this collection and are typical up-to-date dishes.

Purple-tipped globe artichokes ready to harvest (left), a rich variety of fresh vegetables beautifully displayed (above), and a colorful show of wonderful flavoring ingredients, including fresh herbs, chilies, ginger root and spices (right).

A vegetarian diet can provide all the nutrients required for glowing good health, but it is important that meals be balanced to provide sufficient protein. Meat and fish are first-class or complete protein foods, containing all the essential amino acids the body needs for growth and repair. For lacto-vegetarians, protein sources include grains, nuts, legumes, eggs, milk, and cheese, none of which is a complete protein food in itself. To make up such deficiencies as there are, it is important to combine several sources of protein. Combining legumes (a good source of second-class protein) with a grain food, helps to redress the balance, especially if the meal also includes vegetables. This balance occurs naturally in many classic vegetarian dishes.

Wheat is probably the grain most commonly consumed. It comes in many different forms, from whole grain to milled flour. Whole wheat grain, once soaked, can be eaten in the same way as rice. Cracked wheat is the whole grain cracked between rollers, whereas bulgur (bulghur) is cracked wheat that has been hulled and steamed. Both grains can play a useful role in a vegetarian diet. Semolina, made from the starchy part of the grain, is used for gnocchi and couscous. Pasta, bread, cakes, and cookies all contain wheat flour, which is also used as a thickener in cooking.

Other grains include rice in all its varieties, rye kernels and barley, which is often added to soups and stews. Oats in various forms are invaluable for porridge, crumble toppings, in cakes and cookies and for adding to savory dishes. Corn comes in various forms, including hominy (dried corn used in savory dishes) and cornmeal (ground white or yellow corn used for cornbread and tortillas). In Italy, yellow cornmeal is called polenta and is used to make the dish of the same name.

Tofu, also known as soybean curd, should not be overlooked in vegetarian cooking, as it is an excellent source of protein. Made from pressed, puréed soybeans, it is an important ingredient in oriental cooking.

Whether you are an established vegetarian, a recent convert to this way of eating, or a cook who wants to introduce more meat-free dishes into a healthy eating plan, *Classic Vegetarian* will provide endless inspiration for many marvellous meals.

WATERCRESS AND ORANGE SOUP

This is a very healthy and refreshing soup, which is just as good served hot or chilled. It freezes well – transfer to the freezer before adding the cream and use within 2 months.

INGREDIENTS
1 large onion, chopped
1 tablespoon olive oil
2 bunches watercress
grated rind and juice of 1 large orange
1 vegetable bouillon cube
⅔ cup light cream
2 teaspoons cornstarch
salt and ground black pepper
a little heavy cream or yogurt, to garnish
4 orange wedges, to serve

SERVES 4

COOK'S TIP
Wash the watercress only if really necessary; it is often very clean.

1 Place the onion in the oil in a large saucepan and cook gently, stirring occasionally, for 5 minutes, until softened. Trim and discard any large stalks from the watercress, then add the watercress to the onion. Cover the pan and cook the watercress for about 5 minutes, until it is wilted and softened.

2 Add the orange rind and juice. Dissolve the bouillon cube in 2½ cups water, then add to the pan. Cover and simmer for about 10–15 minutes. While the soup is cooking, blend the cream with the cornstarch.

3 Transfer to a food processor or blender and blend the soup thoroughly, then pour through a strainer, if you like. Return to the pan, add the cream and cornstarch mixture, and seasoning to taste.

4 Bring the soup gently back to a boil, stirring until just slightly thickened. Check the seasoning and serve the soup with a swirl of cream or yogurt, and a wedge of orange to squeeze in at the last moment.

GARLIC BAKED TOMATOES

If you can find them, use Italian plum tomatoes, which have a warm, slightly sweet flavor. For large numbers of people you could use whole cherry tomatoes, tossed several times during cooking.

INGREDIENTS
3 tablespoons sweet butter
1 large garlic clove, crushed
1 teaspoon finely grated orange rind
4 firm plum tomatoes, or 2 large beefsteak tomatoes
salt and ground black pepper
fresh basil leaves, to garnish

SERVES 4

COOK'S TIP
Garlic butter is well worth keeping in the freezer. Make as in the recipe, or omit the orange rind and add some chopped fresh parsley. Freeze in thick slices or chunks ready to use, or roll into a sausage shape and wrap in foil, then cut into slices when partly defrosted.

1 In a small bowl, soften the butter with a wooden spoon and blend with the garlic, orange rind, and seasoning. Chill the butter for a few minutes.

2 Preheat the oven to 400°F. Halve the tomatoes crosswise and trim the bases so they stand firmly.

3 Place the tomatoes in an ovenproof dish and spread the garlic butter equally over each tomato half.

4 Bake the garlic tomatoes in the oven for 15–25 minutes, depending on the size of the tomato halves, until they are just tender. Serve the tomatoes, garnished with the fresh basil leaves.

RICE AND CHEESE CROQUETTES

A lthough you can use leftover cooked rice in this dish, freshly cooked rice is easier to work with. The garlicky mayonnaise, aïoli, makes a good dip for crudités too.

INGREDIENTS
½ cup long grain rice, cooked
2 eggs, lightly beaten
3 ounces mozzarella or Bel Paese
cheese, shredded
½ cup fine bread crumbs
salt and ground black pepper
oil, for frying
dill sprigs, to garnish

FOR THE AÏOLI
1 egg yolk
few drops of lemon juice or vinegar
1 large garlic clove, crushed
1 cup olive oil

MAKES ABOUT 16

1 Drain the cooked rice thoroughly and allow to cool slightly, then mix in the eggs, cheese, and seasoning.

2 Mold the rice mixture into 16 equal-size balls and coat in bread crumbs, pressing on the crumbs well. Chill for 20 minutes.

3 Meanwhile, to make the aïoli, put the egg yolk, lemon juice or vinegar, garlic, and seasoning into a bowl and beat together. Gradually whisk in sufficient oil, adding it drop by drop and whisking well between each addition, to give a thick, glossy mayonnaise. Cover and chill before serving.

4 Heat the oil in a frying pan until almost hazy, then cook the rice balls, in two batches, for 4–5 minutes each, or until crisp and golden all over. Drain the rice balls on paper towels and keep warm until required (or reheat in a hot oven) before garnishing with dill sprigs and serving with the aïoli.

LEEK AND STILTON SAMOSAS

These three-cornered packages make great party nibbles, especially if you prepare them well in advance and freeze them ready to cook.

INGREDIENTS

2 leeks, sliced

2 tablespoons milk

1 tablespoon orange juice

¾ cup Stilton cheese, crumbled or diced

8 sheets filo pastry

2 tablespoons butter, melted

ground black pepper

fresh cilantro sprigs, to garnish

MAKES 16

COOK'S TIP

Filo pastry dries out very quickly and then becomes impossible to work with. Cover with a damp dish towel and take out one sheet at a time.

1 Cook the leeks very gently in the milk and orange juice for about 8–10 minutes, until really soft, then season with pepper. Allow the leek mixture to cool slightly before stirring in the Stilton.

2 Preheat the oven to 400°F. Lay one sheet of filo pastry flat, brush it with melted butter and cut in half to make a long oblong strip. Place one-sixteenth of the leek and Stilton mixture in the bottom right-hand corner. Fold the corner point up and over the filling towards the left edge to form a triangular shape.

3 Next, fold the bottom left-hand point up to give a straight bottom edge to the pastry sheet, then fold the pastry triangle over to the right and then up again, so that the filling is completely enclosed. Continue folding up the sheet of pastry and tuck the top flap underneath. Brush with a little butter and place on a baking sheet.

4 Repeat this process for the rest of the pastry and filling mixture, to make about 16 samosas in all.

5 Bake the samosas for 10–15 minutes, until golden brown and crisp. Serve hot, as a snack, garnished with cilantro sprigs as a starter, or hand round at a party as an appetizer with drinks.

SPINACH AND RICOTTA SHELLS

L arge pasta shells are designed to hold a variety of delicious stuffings. Few are more pleasing than this mixture of spinach and ricotta cheese.

INGREDIENTS
12 ounces large pasta shells
1⅞ cup crushed tomatoes
10 ounces frozen chopped spinach, defrosted
1 cup crustless white bread, crumbled
½ cup milk
4 tablespoons olive oil
2¼ cups ricotta cheese
pinch of nutmeg
1 garlic clove, crushed
½ teaspoon black olive paste (optional)
¼ cup freshly shredded Parmesan cheese
2 tablespoons pine nuts
salt and ground black pepper

SERVES 4

COOK'S TIP
Choose a large saucepan when cooking pasta and give it an occasional stir to prevent the shapes from sticking together.

1 Bring a large saucepan of salted water to a boil. Toss in the pasta and cook for about 12 minutes, or until *al dente*. Refresh the pasta under cold water, drain and reserve until needed.

2 Pour the crushed tomatoes into a strainer over a bowl and strain to thicken. Place the spinach in another strainer and press out any excess liquid with a spoon.

3 Place the bread, milk, and 3 tablespoons of the oil in a food processor or blender and combine. Add the spinach and ricotta and season with salt, pepper, and nutmeg.

4 Combine the crushed tomatoes with the garlic, the remaining olive oil, and olive paste, if using. Spread the sauce evenly over the bottom of an ovenproof dish. Spoon the spinach mixture into a pastry bag fitted with a large plain nozzle and fill the pasta shapes (alternatively, fill with a spoon). Arrange the pasta shapes over the sauce.

5 Preheat a moderate broiler. Heat the pasta in a 375°F oven for 10 minutes until warmed through. Sprinkle with Parmesan cheese and pine nuts, and broil until the cheese is browned.

VEGGIE BURGERS

These simple burgers are quick to make and cook, and are ideal for a snack or light meal. Chutneys or pickles, especially homemade ones, are a good accompaniment.

INGREDIENTS
4 ounces cup mushrooms, finely chopped
1 small onion, chopped
1 small zucchini, chopped
1 carrot, chopped
1 ounce unsalted peanuts or cashews
2 cups fresh bread crumbs
2 tablespoons chopped fresh parsley
1 teaspoon yeast extract
fine oatmeal or flour, for shaping
oil, for frying
salt and ground black pepper
crisp salad, to serve

SERVES 4

1 Cook the mushrooms in a nonstick pan without oil, stirring, for 8–10 minutes to remove all the moisture.

2 Process the onion, zucchini, carrot, and nuts in a food processor or blender until beginning to bind together.

3 Stir in the mushrooms, bread crumbs, parsley, yeast extract, and seasoning to taste. With the oatmeal or flour, shape into four burgers (*left*) and chill until firm.

4 Cook the burgers in a nonstick frying pan with very little oil for 8–10 minutes, turning once, until golden brown. Serve hot with a crisp salad.

THAI TOFU CURRY

T hai cooking brings together elements from Malay, Chinese, and Indian cuisine. The favorite Thai flavorings used in this recipe enhance the tofu curry perfectly.

INGREDIENTS
2 × 7-ounce packages tofu, cubed
2 tablespoons light soy sauce
2 tablespoons peanut oil

FOR THE SPICE PASTE
1 small onion, chopped
2 fresh green chilies, seeded and chopped
2 garlic cloves, chopped
1 teaspoon grated fresh ginger root
1 teaspoon grated lime rind
juice of 1 lime or small lemon
2 teaspoons coriander seeds, crushed
2 teaspoons cumin seeds, crushed
3 tablespoons chopped fresh cilantro
1 tablespoon soy sauce
1 teaspoon sugar
1 ounce creamed coconut, dissolved in
⅔ cup boiling water
thin slices of fresh red chili and
lime slices, to garnish
rice, to serve

SERVES 4

1 Toss the tofu cubes in soy sauce and leave to marinate for 15 minutes or so while you prepare the spice paste.

2 Combine the onion, chilies, garlic, ginger, lime rind and juice, coriander and cumin seeds, fresh cilantro, soy sauce, sugar, and coconut in a blender.

3 Heat the oil in a wok or large frying pan until quite hot. Drain the tofu cubes, add to the wok and stir-fry for 5–8 minutes over high heat, until they are well browned on all sides and just firm. Lift out with a slotted spoon and drain on paper towels.

4 Wipe out the wok. Pour in the spice paste and stir well over moderate heat. Return the tofu to the wok and mix it into the spice paste, stirring until it is warmed through. Garnish with the red chili slices and lime slices and serve with rice.

LEEK AND BROCCOLI TARTLETS

Tasty and attractive, these little tartlets with crisp vegetables in a cheese-flavored pastry are also ideal served as an appetizer on their own.

INGREDIENTS
1½ cups flour, sifted
½ cup butter
1 ounce finely shredded pecorino or Parmesan cheese
4–6 tablespoons cold water
flour, for rolling
2 small leeks, sliced
3 ounces tiny broccoli florets
⅔ cup milk
2 eggs
2 tablespoons heavy cream
few pinches of ground mace
salt and ground black pepper
½ ounce sliced almonds, toasted, to garnish

SERVES 4

COOK'S TIP
Cook and freeze the tartlet cases, ready for use at any time. They only need 15 minutes defrosting. Use other colorful, crunchy vegetables when they are in season.

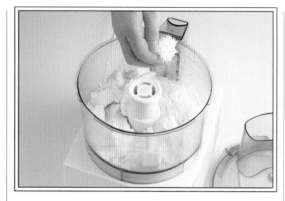

1 Blend together the flour, butter, and cheese in a food processor or blender to give a fine crumb consistency. Add salt and just enough water to bring the pastry together into a ball. Chill for 15 minutes.

2 Preheat the oven to 375°F. Roll out the pastry on a floured surface and use to line four 4-inch tartlet pans. Line the pastry shells with wax paper and fill with dried beans. Bake the tartlets for 15 minutes, then remove the wax paper and beans and cook for 5 minutes more to dry out the bases of the pastry shells.

3 To make the filling, place the leeks and broccoli in a saucepan with the milk and simmer for 2–3 minutes. Strain the milk into a small bowl and whisk in the eggs, cream, mace, and seasoning.

4 Arrange the leeks and broccoli in the pastry shells and pour over the egg mixture. Bake for 20 minutes, or until the filling is just firm. Sprinkle the tartlets with the toasted almonds before serving.

BAKED EGGPLANT SLICES

An unusual way to prepare and cook eggplants, this dish is substantial enough to be served as a light lunch, although it can also be served as an accompaniment to pasta dishes.

INGREDIENTS
3–4 tablespoons olive oil
1 large eggplant
2 large tomatoes, thickly sliced
a few fresh basil leaves, shredded
4 ounces mozzarella cheese, sliced
salt and ground black pepper
fresh basil sprig, to garnish

SERVES 4

1 Preheat the oven to 375°F. Brush a baking sheet with a little oil. Trim the eggplant and cut lengthwise into slices about ¼ inch thick. Arrange the slices on the greased baking sheet.

2 Brush the eggplant slices liberally with the oil and season with salt and pepper. Arrange tomato slices on top of each eggplant slice and then sprinkle with half of the shredded basil.

3 Top with the cheese and another light brushing of oil. Bake for 15 minutes, or until the eggplant is tender and the cheese is bubbling and golden. Serve garnished with the fresh basil sprig.

SPINACH AND POTATO GALETTE

C reamy layers of potato, spinach, and herbs make a warming supper dish. Galette is only one of the many French names for a type of tart.

INGREDIENTS
2 pounds large potatoes
1 pound fresh spinach
2 eggs
1¾ cups low-fat cream cheese
1 tablespoon whole-grain mustard
3 tablespoons chopped fresh herbs, such as chives, parsley, chervil, or sorrel
salt and ground black pepper
salad, to serve

SERVES 6

1 Preheat the oven to 350°F. Line a deep 9-inch cake pan with parchment paper. Place the potatoes in a large pan, cover with cold water, bring to a boil and cook for 10 minutes. Drain the potatoes and let cool slightly before slicing thinly.

2 Wash the spinach and place in a large pan with only the water that is clinging to the leaves. Cover and cook, stirring once, until it has just wilted. Drain well in a strainer and squeeze out all of the excess moisture. Chop the spinach finely.

3 Beat the eggs with the cream cheese and mustard, then stir in the chopped spinach and fresh herbs.

4 Place a layer of the sliced potatoes in the lined pan, arranging them in concentric circles. Cover with a spoonful of the cream cheese mixture and spread out. Continue layering, seasoning with salt and pepper as you go, until all the potatoes and the cream-cheese mixture are used up. Cover the cake pan tightly with a piece of foil and place in a roasting pan.

5 Fill the roasting pan with enough boiling water to come halfway up the sides of the cake pan and bake for 45–50 minutes. Serve hot or cold with a salad.

MIDDLE EASTERN VEGETABLE STEW

A spiced dish of mixed vegetables that can be served as a side-dish or as a main course. Mint and cumin are two of the most popular Middle Eastern flavorings.

INGREDIENTS
3 tablespoons vegetable broth
1 green bell pepper, seeded and sliced
2 zucchini, sliced
2 carrots, sliced
2 celery stalks, sliced
2 potatoes, diced
14-ounce can chopped tomatoes
1 teaspoon chili powder
2 tablespoons chopped fresh mint
1 tablespoon ground cumin
14-ounce can chick-peas, drained
salt and ground black pepper
fresh mint leaves, to garnish

SERVES 4–6

1 Pour the vegetable broth into a large flameproof casserole and heat until boiling, then add the sliced green bell pepper, zucchini, carrots, and celery. Cook over high heat for 2–3 minutes, stirring and turning often, until the vegetables are just beginning to soften.

2 Add the potatoes and tomatoes to the casserole, then season with the chili powder, chopped mint, and cumin. Add the chick-peas and stir to mix the vegetables and spices together, then bring to a boil.

3 Reduce the heat, cover the casserole, and simmer for 30 minutes, or until all the vegetables are tender and cooked through. Season to taste and serve hot, garnished with mint leaves.

COOK'S TIP
Chick-peas are traditional in this type of Middle Eastern dish, but if you prefer, red beans or navy beans can be used instead.

APPLE, ONION, AND GRUYERE TART

T he grated apple adds a subtle flavor to this quiche filling. Other hard cheeses, such as Cheddar, may be used instead of Gruyère.

INGREDIENTS
2 cups flour
1 teaspoon mustard powder
6 tablespoons soft margarine
6 tablespoons finely shredded
Gruyère cheese
2 tablespoons water
crisp salad, to serve

FOR THE FILLING
2 tablespoons butter
1 large onion, finely chopped
2 small eating apples, peeled and grated
2 large eggs
⅔ cup heavy cream
¼ teaspoon dried mixed herbs
½ teaspoon mustard powder
4 ounces Gruyère cheese
salt and ground black pepper

SERVES 4–6

1 To make the pastry, sift the flour, salt, and mustard into a large bowl. Rub in the margarine and cheese until the mixture forms soft crumbs. Add the water and mix to a dough. Chill, covered, for 30 minutes.

2 Meanwhile, to make the filling, melt the butter in a pan, add the onion and cook gently for 10 minutes, stirring occasionally, until softened but not browned. Stir in the apple and cook for 2–3 minutes, then remove from the heat and leave to cool.

3 Preheat the oven to 400°F. Roll out the pastry and use it to line a lightly greased 8-inch fluted quiche pan. Chill in the refrigerator for 20 minutes. Line the pastry shell with wax paper and fill with dried beans. Bake for 20 minutes.

4 Beat together the eggs, cream, herbs, mustard, and seasoning. Grate three-quarters of the cheese and stir into the egg mixture, then slice the remaining cheese and set aside. When the pastry is cooked, remove the paper and beans and pour in the egg mixture.

5 Arrange the sliced cheese over the top. Reduce the oven heat to 375°F. Return the tart to the oven and cook for 20 minutes, until the filling is just firm. Serve hot or warm with a crisp, green salad.

GREEN LENTILS WITH SWEET ONIONS

A delicious, wholesome dish with a sweet flavor, topped with crunchy cashews for added bite. The dark blue-green Puy lentils from France would be a good choice.

INGREDIENTS
2 tablespoons sunflower oil
1 small onion, chopped
2 garlic cloves, crushed
1 cup green lentils
2½ cups vegetable broth
⅔ cup red wine
1 teaspoon chopped fresh sage, or a pinch of dried sage
8 ounces pearl onions, peeled
2 tablespoons butter
4 tablespoons soft light brown sugar
salt and ground black pepper
½ cup salted cashews and thyme sprigs, to garnish

SERVES 3–4

1 Heat the oil in a flameproof casserole and fry the onion and garlic until soft. Add the lentils (*left*) and fry gently for 3 minutes.

2 Stir in the broth, red wine, sage, and seasoning. Bring to a boil. Cover and simmer gently for 20 minutes, stirring occasionally, until the lentils are tender. Add more liquid if necessary.

3 Meanwhile, in a small frying pan, gently fry the onions with the butter and sugar for 5–7 minutes, until the sugar begins to caramelize and the onions are just tender. Stir occasionally.

4 Serve the lentils sprinkled with the cashews, garnished with thyme sprigs, and accompanied by the onions.

MUSHROOM POPOVERS

Individual Yorkshire puddings with a quick-and-easy mushroom filling will be a popular choice with the whole family.

INGREDIENTS
1 egg
1 cup flour
1¼ cups milk
pinch of salt
oil, for greasing

FOR THE FILLING
1 tablespoon sunflower oil
4 ounces mushrooms, sliced
few drops of lemon juice
2 teaspoons chopped fresh parsley or thyme
¼ red bell pepper, seeded and chopped
salt and ground black pepper
shredded fresh basil and fresh basil leaves, to garnish

SERVES 4

1 To make the popovers, whisk the egg and flour together and gradually add a little milk to blend, then whisk in the rest of the milk to make a smooth batter. Add a pinch of salt and leave the batter to stand for at least 10–20 minutes.

2 Preheat the oven to 375°F. Pour a little oil into the base of eight popover pans and heat through in the oven for about 4–5 minutes. Add the batter to the hot pans and cook for 20 minutes, or until the batter puddings are well risen and crispy.

COOK'S TIP
For perfect batter, it is important that both the fat and the oven are very hot otherwise the batter will be heavy, tough, or soggy. When a batter doesn't rise properly, the mixture is probably too thin.

3 Meanwhile, to make the filling, heat the oil and sauté the mushrooms with the lemon juice, herbs, and seasoning until most of the liquid has evaporated. Add the red bell pepper at the last minute so that it keeps its crunch. Taste for seasoning.

4 Spoon the mushroom filling into the hot popover cases, sprinkle over the basil and serve immediately.

BROCCOLI AND CHESTNUT TERRINE

This attractive terrine, which is equally good hot or cold, makes a splendid main course for a dinner party. It is also perfect for a picnic.

INGREDIENTS

1 pound broccoli, cut into small florets
8 ounces cooked chestnuts,
roughly chopped
1 cup fresh whole wheat bread crumbs
4 tablespoons low-fat plain yogurt
2 tablespoons Parmesan cheese,
finely shredded
salt, grated nutmeg, and ground
black pepper
2 eggs, beaten
new potatoes and salad, to serve

SERVES 4–6

1 Preheat the oven to 350°F. Line a 2-pound loaf pan with parchment paper.

2 Blanch or steam the broccoli florets for 3–4 minutes until just tender. Drain thoroughly. Reserve about a quarter of the smallest florets and chop the rest finely.

3 Place the chopped chestnuts, with the bread crumbs, yogurt, and Parmesan in a large bowl and season to taste with salt, nutmeg, and pepper. Fold in the chopped broccoli, the reserved florets, and the beaten eggs and stir until thoroughly combined.

4 Spoon the broccoli mixture into the pan. Place in a roasting pan and pour in boiling water to come halfway up the sides of the loaf pan. Bake for 20–25 minutes. Remove from the oven and tip out on to a plate. Serve sliced, with potatoes and salad.

CHICK-PEAS AND ARTICHOKES AU GRATIN

A very quick and extremely tasty dish, with an unusual combination of flavors that will impress friends and family alike.

INGREDIENTS

14-ounce can chick-peas, drained
14-ounce can black-eyed peas, drained
4½-ounce jar artichoke antipasti (or canned artichoke hearts, chopped, plus a little olive oil)
1 red bell pepper, seeded and chopped
1 garlic clove, crushed
1 tablespoon chopped fresh parsley
1 teaspoon lemon juice
⅔ cup sour cream
1 egg yolk
½ cup shredded Cheddar cheese
salt and ground black pepper

SERVES 4

1 Preheat the oven to 350°F. Mix together the chick-peas, black-eyed peas, artichoke antipasti or artichoke hearts, and red bell pepper.

2 Stir in as much of the dressing from the antipasti, or oil if using artichoke hearts, as necessary to moisten the mixture. Stir in the garlic, parsley, lemon juice and season.

3 Mix together the sour cream, egg yolk, cheese, and seasoning. Spoon the mixture over the vegetables (*left*) and bake for 25–30 minutes, or until golden.

BROCCOLI-CAULIFLOWER GRATIN

Broccoli and cauliflower make an attractive combination, and this sauce is much lighter than the classic cheese sauce.

INGREDIENTS
1 small cauliflower, about 9 ounces
1 small head broccoli, about 9 ounces
salt
½ cup low-fat plain yogurt
1 cup shredded Cheddar cheese
1 teaspoon whole-grain mustard
2 tablespoons whole wheat bread crumbs
salt and ground black pepper

SERVES 4

COOK'S TIP
When preparing the cauliflower and broccoli, discard the tougher part of the stalks, then break the florets into even-size pieces, so they cook evenly.

1 Break the cauliflower and broccoli into florets and cook in lightly salted boiling water for 8–10 minutes, until just tender. Drain well and transfer to a flameproof dish.

2 In a bowl, mix together the yogurt, cheese, and mustard, then season the mixture with pepper and spoon evenly over the cauliflower and broccoli.

3 Sprinkle the bread crumbs over the top of the sauce and place the dish under a preheated hot broiler and cook until golden brown and bubbling. Serve hot.

LEMON CARROT SALAD

Enjoy this tangy, colorful, and refreshing salad at any time. If you like, add a sprinkling of toasted sesame seeds just before serving.

INGREDIENTS
1 pound baby carrots
grated rind and juice of ½ lemon
1 tablespoon soft light brown sugar
4 tablespoons sunflower oil
1 teaspoon hazelnut or sesame oil
1 teaspoon chopped fresh oregano, and a
fresh oregano sprig, to garnish
salt and ground black pepper

SERVES 4–6

COOK'S TIP
Other root vegetables can be used in this salad. For instance, you could try replacing half of the carrot with rutabaga, or use celery root or kohlrabi instead.

1 Finely grate the carrots and place them in a large bowl. Stir in the lemon rind, 2 tablespoons of the lemon juice, the sugar, and oils, and mix well.

2 Add more lemon juice and seasoning to taste, then sprinkle on the oregano, toss lightly, and leave the salad for 1 hour before serving, garnished with the oregano sprig.

CRISP FRUITY SALAD

C risp lettuce, tangy cheese, sweet grapes, crunchy pieces of apple, and garlic croûtons make this an interesting and refreshing salad.

INGREDIENTS
½ Bibb lettuce
3 ounces grapes, seeded and halved
½ cup shredded mature Cheddar cheese
1 large eating apple, cored and
thinly sliced
3 tablespoons garlic croûtons, to garnish

FOR THE VINAIGRETTE
1 tablespoon French mustard
1 tablespoon white wine vinegar
pinch of sugar
4 tablespoons sunflower oil
salt and ground black pepper

SERVES 4

1 Tear the lettuce leaves into bite-size pieces and place in a salad bowl. Add the grapes, cheese, and apple.

2 To make the vinaigrette dressing, put the mustard, vinegar, sugar, and seasoning into a small bowl and whisk together with a fork to combine. Gradually add the oil, whisking to emulsify.

3 Pour the dressing over the salad *(left)*. Mix well and serve at once, sprinkled with garlic croûtons.

WATERCRESS AND POTATO SALAD

New potatoes are equally delicious hot or cold, and this colorful, nutritious salad is an ideal way of making the most of them.

INGREDIENTS

1 pound small new potatoes, unpeeled
1 bunch watercress
1½ cups cherry tomatoes, halved
2 tablespoons pumpkin seeds
3 tablespoons low-fat ricotta cheese
1 tablespoon cider vinegar
1 teaspoon brown sugar
salt and paprika

SERVES 4

COOK'S TIP
If you are packing this salad for a picnic, take the dressing in the jar and toss in just before serving.

1 Cook the potatoes in lightly salted, boiling water until just tender, then drain and leave to cool.

2 Put the potatoes, watercress, cherry tomatoes, and pumpkin seeds into a bowl and toss together.

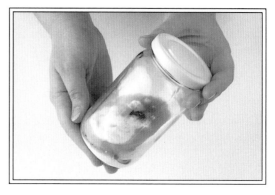

3 Place the ricotta cheese, vinegar, sugar, salt, and paprika in a screw-top jar and shake well to mix. Pour the dressing over the salad just before serving.

VARIATION
Potato salad is an essential part of summer eating, but there are endless ways to ring the changes to this simple recipe. The one essential is a good waxy salad potato – as freshly dug as possible – they taste so much better that way. Young spinach leaves or the peppery-flavored arugula can be used instead of the watercress, or you can use any combination of two, or all three of them. Sour cream can be used instead of ricotta cheese and balsamic vinegar, with its more mellow flavor substituted for the cider vinegar.

SPICY BAKED POTATOES

Baked potatoes are a universal favorite. Here, a combination of fresh ginger and warming aromatic spices add an unusual piquant flavor.

INGREDIENTS
2 large baking potatoes
1 teaspoon sunflower oil
1 small onion, finely chopped
1-inch piece fresh ginger root, shredded
1 teaspoon ground cumin
1 teaspoon ground coriander
½ teaspoon ground turmeric
garlic salt, to taste
plain yogurt and fresh cilantro sprigs, to serve

SERVES 2–4

1 Preheat the oven to 375°F. Prick the potatoes all over with a fork. Bake for 40 minutes, or until soft.

2 Cut the potatoes lengthwise in half, scoop out the flesh, and set aside on a plate. Heat the oil in a large nonstick frying pan, add the onion and sauté for a few minutes to soften.

3 Add the ginger, cumin, coriander, and turmeric to the onion and stir over low heat for about 2 minutes. Add the potato flesh and garlic salt, to taste, and stir to coat thoroughly with the spice mixture.

4 Cook the potato mixture for another 2 minutes, stirring occasionally. Spoon the mixture back into the potato shells and top each potato with a spoonful of yogurt and a cilantro sprig. Serve hot.

STIR-FRIED FLORETS WITH HAZELNUTS

rich hazelnut sauce transforms crunchy cauliflower and broccoli florets into a special vegetable dish.

INGREDIENTS
6 ounces cauliflower, broken into florets
6 ounces broccoli, broken into florets
1 tablespoon sunflower oil
½ cup hazelnuts, finely chopped
4 tablespoons crème fraîche or
sour cream
salt and ground black pepper
chili powder or finely chopped
red bell pepper, to garnish

SERVES 4

1 Make sure the cauliflower and broccoli florets are all of a similar size. Heat the oil in a large frying pan or wok and toss the florets over high heat for 1 minute.

2 Reduce the heat and continue to stir-fry for another 5 minutes, then add the hazelnuts and season to taste.

3 When the cauliflower and broccoli florets are crisp and nearly tender, stir in the crème fraîche or sour cream and heat gently until the mixture is just warmed through. Serve the florets immediately, garnished with a fine sprinkling of chili powder or finely chopped red bell pepper.

COOK'S TIP
The crisper these florets are the better, so cook them just long enough to make them piping hot, and give them time to absorb all the flavors.

TORTELLINI WITH CHEESE SAUCE

H ere is a very quick way of making a delicious cheese sauce without all the usual effort. But do eat it when really hot before the sauce starts to thicken.

INGREDIENTS
1 pound fresh tortellini
4 ounces ricotta or cream cheese
4–6 tablespoons milk
½ cup shredded St. Paulin or
mozzarella cheese
½ cup shredded Parmesan cheese
2 garlic cloves, crushed
2 tablespoons chopped fresh mixed herbs,
such as parsley, chives, basil, or oregano,
and sprigs, to garnish
salt and ground black pepper

SERVES 4

1 Cook the pasta according to the manufacturer's instructions, in boiling, salted water, stirring occasionally.

2 Meanwhile, gently melt the ricotta or cream cheese with the milk in a large saucepan. When blended, stir in the St. Paulin or mozzarella cheese, half of the Parmesan, and the garlic and chopped herbs.

3 Drain the cooked pasta and add to the sauce. Stir well and cook gently for 1–2 minutes to melt the cheese. Season, and garnish with herb sprigs. Serve sprinkled with the remaining Parmesan cheese.

PASTA WITH CHICK-PEA SAUCE

A n unusual combination, the chick-peas give this pasta dish a delightful crunchiness. This is a quick, easy supper dish.

INGREDIENTS
1 teaspoon olive oil
1 small onion, finely chopped
1 garlic clove, crushed
1 celery stalk, finely chopped
15-ounce can chick-peas, drained
1 cup ready-made tomato sauce
8 ounces pasta shapes
salt and ground black pepper
chopped fresh parsley, to garnish

SERVES 4

1 Heat the oil in a nonstick pan and sauté the onion, garlic, and celery until softened but not browned. Stir in the chick-peas and the tomato sauce, then cover and simmer for about 15 minutes.

2 Cook the pasta in a large pan of boiling lightly salted water according to the manufacturer's instructions. Drain and toss with the sauce (*left*), then season to taste. Sprinkle with chopped fresh parsley and serve at once.

PASTA WITH SPRING VEGETABLES

Known as *pasta primavera,* this classic dish makes the most of fresh vegetables. For a lighter sauce, use strained plain yogurt instead of the heavy cream.

INGREDIENTS
4 ounces broccoli florets
4 ounces baby leeks
8 ounces asparagus
1 small fennel bulb
4 ounces fresh or frozen peas
3 tablespoons butter
1 shallot, chopped
3 tablespoons chopped fresh mixed herbs,
such as parsley, thyme, and sage
1¼ cups heavy cream
12 ounces penne
salt and ground black pepper
freshly shredded Parmesan cheese,
to serve

SERVES 4

1 Divide the broccoli florets into tiny sprigs. Cut the leeks and asparagus into 2-inch lengths. Trim the fennel bulb and remove any tough outer leaves. Cut into wedges, leaving the layers attached at the root ends so the pieces stay intact.

2 Cook each vegetable separately in boiling salted water until just tender – use the same water for each vegetable. Drain well and keep warm.

3 Melt the butter in a separate pan, add the chopped shallot and cook, stirring occasionally, until softened but not browned. Stir in the herbs and cream and gently cook for a few minutes, until the sauce is slightly thickened.

4 Meanwhile, cook the pasta in boiling salted water for 10 minutes. Drain and add to the sauce with the vegetables. Toss and season with pepper.

5 Serve the pasta hot with a sprinkling of freshly shredded Parmesan cheese.

EGGPLANT LASAGNE

rich and filling supper dish that needs only to be served with a light green salad. It freezes very well.

INGREDIENTS
3 eggplants, sliced
5 tablespoons olive oil
2 large onions, finely chopped
2 × 14-ounce cans chopped tomatoes
1 teaspoon dried mixed herbs
2–3 garlic cloves, crushed
6 sheets fresh lasagne
salt and ground black pepper
fresh sage sprigs, to garnish

FOR THE CHEESE SAUCE
2 tablespoons butter
2 tablespoons flour
1¼ cups milk
½ teaspoon English mustard
8 tablespoons shredded mature Cheddar cheese
1 tablespoon shredded Parmesan cheese

SERVES 4

COOK'S TIP
To freeze, cook for only 20 minutes, cool, then put in the freezer. Reheat at 375°F for 35–45 minutes.

1 Layer the sliced eggplant in a colander, sprinkling lightly with salt between each layer. Leave to stand for 1 hour, then rinse well and pat dry on paper towels.

2 Heat 4 tablespoons of the oil in a large pan, fry the eggplant slices on both sides, then drain on paper towels. Add the remaining oil to the pan, cook the onions for 5 minutes, then stir in the tomatoes, herbs, garlic, and seasoning. Bring to a boil and simmer, covered, for 30 minutes. Preheat the oven to 400°F.

3 Meanwhile, to make the cheese sauce, melt the butter in a pan, add the flour and cook for 1 minute, stirring. Gradually stir in the milk. Bring to a boil and simmer for 2 minutes. Remove from the heat and stir in the mustard and cheeses. Season.

4 Arrange half of the eggplant slices in an ovenproof dish and add half of the tomato sauce. Top with three sheets of lasagne. Repeat the layers. Add the cheese sauce, and bake for 30 minutes. Garnish with the sage sprigs and serve at once.

GOLDEN VEGETABLE PAELLA

Wild rice is actually not a rice at all but a wild native grass. It gives a nutty flavor and crunchy texture to this colorful dish.

INGREDIENTS

pinch of saffron strands or 1 teaspoon
ground turmeric
3⅔ cups hot vegetable broth
6 tablespoons olive oil
2 large onions, sliced
3 garlic cloves, chopped
1½ cups long grain rice
⅓ cup wild rice
6 ounces pumpkin or butternut
squash, chopped
6 ounces carrots, cut into matchsticks
1 yellow bell pepper, seeded and sliced
4 tomatoes, peeled and chopped
4 ounces oyster mushrooms, quartered
salt and ground black pepper
strips of red, yellow, and green
bell pepper, to garnish

SERVES 4

1 Place the saffron, if using, in a small bowl with 3–4 tablespoons of the hot vegetable broth. Stand for 5 minutes. Heat the oil in a large, heavy-based frying pan. Fry the onions and garlic for 2–3 minutes.

2 Add the rices and toss for 2–3 minutes until coated in oil. Add the remaining broth to the pan with the pumpkin or squash and the saffron strands and their liquid, or the turmeric. Stir as the mixture comes to a boil, then reduce the heat to very low. Cover the pan with a lid or foil and cook very gently for about 15 minutes. (Avoid stirring as this lets out the steam and moisture and the rices will cook unevenly.)

3 Add the carrots, bell pepper, tomatoes, and seasoning, replace the lid and cook over gentle heat for another 5 minutes, or until the rice is almost tender.

4 Add the oyster mushrooms, check the seasoning and cook, uncovered, for just long enough for the mushrooms to soften, without letting the paella stick. Top with the strips of bell pepper and serve at once.

TAGLIATELLE WITH PEA SAUCE, ASPARAGUS, AND FAVA BEANS

A creamy pea and sage sauce combines wonderfully with the crunchy young vegetables in this light, summery pasta dish.

INGREDIENTS
1 tablespoon olive oil
1 garlic clove, crushed
6 scallions, sliced
1 cup frozen baby peas, defrosted
12 ounces fresh young asparagus
2 tablespoons chopped fresh sage, plus
extra leaves to garnish
finely grated rind of 2 lemons
1¾ cups vegetable broth or water
8 ounces frozen fava beans, defrosted
1 pound tagliatelle
4 tablespoons low-fat yogurt

SERVES 4

1 Heat the oil in a pan. Add the garlic and scallions and cook gently for 2–3 minutes until softened.

2 Add the peas, a third of the asparagus, the sage, lemon rind, and broth or water. Bring to a boil, reduce the heat and simmer for 10 minutes, until tender. Process in a blender or food processor until smooth.

3 Meanwhile, remove the outer skins from the fava beans and discard. Cut the remaining asparagus into 2-inch lengths, discarding any tough fibrous stems, and blanch in boiling water for 2 minutes.

4 Cook the tagliatelle in a pan of boiling salted water for about 10 minutes until *al dente*. Drain well.

5 Add the cooked asparagus and skinned beans to the sauce and reheat. Stir in the yogurt. Add the sauce to the tagliatelle and toss together. Garnish with a few extra sage leaves and serve immediately.

POLENTA AND BAKED TOMATOES

A staple of northern Italy, polenta is a nourishing, filling food, served here with a delicious fresh tomato and olive topping.

INGREDIENTS

8 cups water
1¼ pounds quick-cook polenta
oil, for greasing
12 large ripe plum tomatoes, sliced
4 garlic cloves, thinly sliced
*2 tablespoons chopped fresh
oregano or marjoram*
1 cup black olives, pitted
salt and ground black pepper
2 tablespoons olive oil

SERVES 4–6

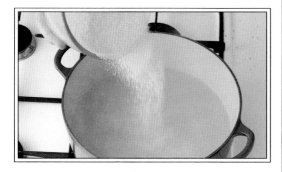

1 Pour the water into a large saucepan and bring to a boil. Add the polenta. Press out any lumps with a wooden spoon, then simmer for 5 minutes, until thickened.

2 Remove the pan from the heat and pour the polenta into a 9 × 13-inch jelly roll pan. Carefully smooth out the surface of the polenta with a metal spatula until level, and leave to cool.

3 Preheat the oven to 350°F. With a 3-inch round pastry cutter, stamp out about 12 rounds of the cooled polenta. Remove the rounds from the jelly roll pan with the metal spatula and arrange them in a lightly oiled ovenproof dish so that they slightly overlap one another.

4 Layer the tomatoes, garlic, oregano or marjoram, and olives on top of the polenta, seasoning the layers as you go. Sprinkle with the olive oil and bake uncovered for 30–35 minutes. Serve immediately.

RICE WITH SEEDS AND SPICES

A change from plain boiled rice, this dish is a flavorful accompaniment to serve with spicy curries. Basmati rice gives the best texture and flavor, but you can use ordinary long grain rice instead.

INGREDIENTS
1 teaspoon sunflower oil
½ teaspoon ground turmeric
6 cardamom pods, lightly crushed
1 teaspoon coriander seeds,
lightly crushed
1 garlic clove, crushed
1 cup basmati rice
1⅔ cups vegetable broth
½ cup plain yogurt
1 tablespoon toasted sunflower seeds
1 tablespoon toasted sesame seeds
salt and ground black pepper
fresh cilantro sprigs, to garnish

SERVES 4

1 Heat the oil in a large nonstick frying pan and add the tumeric, cardamom pods, crushed coriander seeds, and garlic. Sauté for about 1 minute, stirring all the time.

2 Add the rice and vegetable broth, bring to a boil, then cover and simmer for 15 minutes, or until just tender.

3 Stir in the yogurt and the toasted sunflower and sesame seeds. Adjust the seasoning and serve hot, garnished with the fresh cilantro sprigs.

COOK'S TIP
Seeds of every sort are particularly rich in minerals, so they are a good addition to all kinds of dishes. Light roasting improves their flavor.

PENNE WITH BROCCOLI AND CHILI

Make this spicy dish as mild or hot as you like by varying the amount of sliced red chili.

INGREDIENTS
12 ounces penne
1 pound broccoli, broken into
small florets
2 tablespoons vegetable broth
1 garlic clove, crushed
1 small red chili, sliced, or ½ teaspoon
chili sauce
4 tablespoons plain low-fat yogurt
2 tablespoons toasted pine nuts
salt and ground black pepper

SERVES 4

1 Add the pasta to a pan of boiling salted water. Place the broccoli in a steamer over the top. Cover and cook for about 8–10 minutes until both are tender. Drain.

2 Pour the vegetable broth into a large saucepan and bring just to a boil. Add the crushed garlic and chili or chili sauce. Stir over low heat for 2–3 minutes.

3 Stir the broccoli, pasta, and yogurt into the spice mixture. Adjust the seasoning. Transfer to warmed individual plates, sprinkle with the nuts, and serve at once.

50

TAGLIATELLE WITH HAZELNUT PESTO

For the health conscious, it is good news that hazelnuts are lower in fat than other nuts. In this recipe, they are used as an alternative to pine nuts in the pesto sauce.

INGREDIENTS
2 garlic cloves, crushed
1 ounce fresh basil leaves
1 ounce hazelnuts
⅞ cup skim milk soft cheese
8 ounces dried tagliatelle, or 1 pound fresh tagliatelle
salt and ground black pepper

SERVES 4

1 Place the garlic, basil, hazelnuts, and cheese in a food processor or blender and process to a thick paste, or pound to a paste using a pestle and mortar.

2 Cook the tagliatelle in a large saucepan of lightly salted boiling water for about 10 minutes or until *al dente*. Drain the tagliatelle thoroughly.

3 Spoon the hazelnut pesto into the hot pasta, tossing until melted. Transfer to warmed individual plates, sprinkle with pepper, and serve immediately.

DEEP-PAN VEGETABLE PIZZA

A glorious mix of fresh vegetables tops this luxurious deep-pan pizza. Vary the vegetables according to what is in season, but aim for a variety of colors, shapes, and textures.

INGREDIENTS
FOR THE PIZZA DOUGH
6 ounces flour
1 teaspoon salt
½ package fast-rising dried yeast
1 tablespoon oil
about ½ cup warm water

FOR THE TOPPING
½ cup canned creamed mushrooms
2 ounces each cooked green beans,
cauliflower florets, and baby corn
6–8 cherry tomatoes, halved
2–3 pieces sun-dried tomato in oil,
finely chopped
2 tablespoons ready-made tomato sauce
½ cup shredded blue cheese
oil, for brushing
salt and ground black pepper

SERVES 4

1 To make the pizza dough, mix together the flour, salt, and yeast in a large bowl. Stir in the oil and enough water to mix to a soft dough. Knead for 5 minutes until smooth. Stretch out the dough and use to line a 7-inch deep pizza pan, or a shallow loose-based cake pan. Spread the pizza base with the mushrooms.

2 Arrange the cooked vegetables neatly over the top and sprinkle with seasoning. Add the halved tomatoes and the sun-dried tomatoes cut into tiny pieces.

3 Drizzle over the tomato sauce and sprinkle on the cheese. Brush with oil where necessary and sprinkle with more seasoning. Leave in a warm place for the dough to rise up to the top of the pan.

4 Meanwhile, preheat the oven to 425°F. Bake the pizza for 15–20 minutes, until golden all over, bubbling in the middle, and becoming quite crispy at the edges.

PIZZA WITH FRESH VEGETABLES

T his pizza can be made with any combination of fresh seasonal vegetables. It is best to blanch or sauté them before baking.

INGREDIENTS
3 cups flour
1 teaspoon salt
pinch of sugar
1 package fast-rising dried yeast
about 1 cup warm water

FOR THE TOPPING
14 ounces peeled plum tomatoes,
fresh or canned, drained
8 ounces broccoli florets
8 ounces fresh asparagus, cut into
1–1½-inch pieces
12 small zucchini, sliced lengthwise
5 tablespoons olive oil-
⅓ cup shelled peas, fresh or frozen
4 scallions, sliced
3 ounces mozzarella cheese, diced
10 leaves fresh basil, torn into pieces
2 garlic cloves, finely chopped
salt and ground black pepper

MAKES 4

1 To make the dough, sift the flour and salt and stir in the sugar and yeast. Add enough water to mix to a soft dough. Knead for 5 minutes. Cover and leave in a warm place for about 1 hour, or until doubled.

2 To make the topping, strain the tomatoes through the medium holes of a food mill, scraping in all the pulp. Blanch the broccoli, asparagus, and zucchini for 2–3 minutes. Drain well. Heat 2 tablespoons of the oil, add the peas and scallions and cook for about 5 minutes.

3 Preheat the oven to 475°F. Roll out the dough to make four 8-inch bases and place on baking sheets.

4 Spread the puréed tomatoes over the pizza bases, leaving the rims uncovered. Spread the other vegetables evenly over the tomatoes. Sprinkle with the mozzarella cheese, fresh basil, chopped garlic, salt and pepper, and the remaining olive oil. Bake the pizzas for about 20 minutes, or until the crusts are golden brown, the vegetables are tender, and the cheese has melted.

CRACKED WHEAT WITH FENNEL

Combining sweet and savory flavors, this unusually crunchy salad is mixed with a delightful garlic vinaigrette dressing.

INGREDIENTS

¾ cup cracked or bulgur wheat

1 large fennel bulb, finely chopped

4 ounces green beans, chopped and blanched

1 small orange

1 garlic clove, crushed

2–3 tablespoons sunflower oil

1 tablespoon white wine vinegar

salt and ground black pepper

½ red or orange bell pepper, seeded and finely chopped, to garnish

SERVES 4

1 Place the cracked or bulgur wheat in a bowl and cover with boiling water. Leave for 10–15 minutes, stirring occasionally. When doubled in size, drain well and squeeze out any excess water.

2 While the wheat is still slightly warm, stir in the chopped fennel and the green beans. Finely grate the orange rind into a small bowl. Peel and segment the orange and stir into the salad.

3 Add the garlic, oil, vinegar, and seasoning to the orange rind, and mix thoroughly. Pour over the salad and mix well. Chill the salad for about 1–2 hours, before serving garnished with the chopped bell pepper.

CHILLED CHOCOLATE SLICE

This is a very rich pudding, perfect for using up leftovers. You don't need to eat it all at once as it keeps extremely well.

INGREDIENTS
½ cup butter, melted, plus extra
for greasing
8 ounces ginger cookies, finely crushed
2 ounces day-old sponge cake crumbs
4–5 tablespoons orange juice
½ cup pitted dates, warmed
¼ cup finely chopped nuts
6 ounces bitter chocolate
1¼ cups whipping cream
grated chocolate and confectioner's
sugar, to decorate
1 orange, cut into segments, to serve

SERVES 6–8

1 Brush an 7-inch loose-bottomed quiche pan with a little of the butter. Put the remaining butter into a bowl with the cookie crumbs and mix together. Pack the crumb mixture evenly round the sides and base of the quiche pan, pressing with the back of a spoon. Chill the base for 15 minutes while preparing the filling.

2 Put the cake crumbs into a bowl with the orange juice and leave to soak. Mash the dates with a fork, add the cake crumbs and the chopped nuts and mix well.

3 In a small pan, melt the bitter chocolate with 3–4 tablespoons of the cream. Softly whip the remaining cream, then fold in the melted chocolate mixture.

4 Stir the cream and chocolate mixture into the crumbs and mix well. Pour into the cookie crust, mark into portions, and leave to set. Sprinkle over the grated chocolate and dust with confectioner's sugar. Cut into wedges and serve with the orange segments.

> **COOK'S TIP**
> To make cookie crumbs, either grind the cookies in a food processor or a blender or place them in a strong plastic bag and crush them with a rolling pin.

APPLE AND APRICOT CRUMBLE

Lightly cook the fruit base first for the best results. That way you'll get a delicious contrast between the soft fruit and its crunchy topping.

INGREDIENTS
15-ounce can apricot halves in natural juice
1 pound cooking apples, peeled and sliced
sugar, to taste (optional)
grated rind of 1 orange
ground nutmeg, to taste

FOR THE TOPPING
1¾ cups flour
½ cup rolled oats
10 tablespoons butter or sunflower margarine
¼ cup soft brown sugar
raw sugar, to sprinkle

SERVES 4–6

1 Preheat the oven to 375°F. Drain the apricot halves in a colander, reserving a little of the juice.

2 Put the sliced apples into a large saucepan and pour in a little of the reserved apricot juice and sugar to taste, if liked. Simmer gently for 5 minutes to cook the apple pieces lightly.

3 Transfer the apples to an ovenproof pie dish and add the apricot halves and orange rind. Add a little ground nutmeg to taste. Stir to combine the two fruits.

4 To make the topping, rub the flour, oats and butter or margarine together until they form fine crumbs. (You can use a food processor or blender, if you prefer.) Mix in the soft brown sugar.

5 Sprinkle the crumble over the fruit, spreading it evenly. Sprinkle with a little raw sugar. Bake for about 30 minutes, until the crumble is golden and crisp. Allow the crumble to cool slightly before serving.

SPICED PEARS IN CIDER

Any variety of pear can be used for cooking, but firm pears are best for this recipe, as they do not break up easily – Beurré Bosc is a good choice.

INGREDIENTS
4 firm pears
1 cup dry cider
thinly pared strip of lemon rind
1 cinnamon stick
2 tablespoons brown sugar
1 teaspoon arrowroot
1 tablespoon cold water
ground cinnamon, to sprinkle
heavy cream, to serve (optional)

SERVES 4

1 Peel the pears thinly, leaving them whole with the stems on. Place in a pan with the cider, lemon rind, and cinnamon stick. Simmer for 15–20 minutes, or until tender.

2 Lift out the pears. Boil the syrup, uncovered, to reduce it by about half. Remove the lemon rind and cinnamon stick, then stir in the sugar.

3 Mix the arrowroot with the water in a small bowl until smooth, then stir into the syrup (*right*). Bring the mixture to a boil and stir constantly over the heat until thickened and clear.

4 Pour the sauce over the pears and sprinkle with ground cinnamon. Leave to cool slightly, then serve warm, with heavy cream if you like.

RASPBERRY AND PASSIONFRUIT SWIRLS

I f passionfruit are not available, this simple dessert can be made with raspberries alone. Over-ripe, slightly soft raspberries can be used in this recipe.

INGREDIENTS
2½ cups raspberries
2 passionfruit
1⅔ cups low-fat ricotta cheese
2 tablespoons sugar
raspberries and fresh mint sprigs,
to decorate

SERVES 4

1 Mash the raspberries in a bowl with a fork until the juice runs. Scoop the passionfruit pulp into a separate bowl, add the ricotta cheese and sugar and mix well.

2 Put alternate spoonfuls of the raspberry pulp and the ricotta cheese and passionfruit mixture into 4 stemmed glasses, or other serving glasses.

3 Stir lightly to create a swirled effect. Chill the desserts until ready to serve. To decorate, place one whole raspberry and a sprig of fresh mint in the center of each.

APPLE AND MINT HAZELNUT SHORTCAKE

Apple and mint make an unusual filling for this nutty shortcake dessert, but you can use any summer fruit, such as raspberries or strawberries, if you prefer.

INGREDIENTS
1 cup whole-wheat flour
4 tablespoons ground hazelnuts
4 tablespoons confectioner's sugar, sifted
10 tablespoons sweet butter
or margarine
flour, for rolling
3 sharp eating apples
1 teaspoon lemon juice
1–2 tablespoons sugar, to taste
1 tablespoon chopped fresh mint, or
1 teaspoon dried mint
1 cup whipping cream or crème fraîche
few drops of vanilla extract
mint sprigs and whole hazelnuts,
to decorate

SERVES 8–10

COOK'S TIP
The shortcake bases can be made in advance, left to cool, and stored for 7–10 days in an airtight container.

1 Process the flour, hazelnuts, and confectioner's sugar with the butter in a food processor or blender in short bursts, or rub the butter into the dry ingredients until they come together. (Don't overwork the mixture.) Bring the dough together, adding a very little iced water if necessary. Knead the dough briefly, then wrap in wax paper and chill for 30 minutes.

2 Preheat the oven to 325°F. Cut the dough in half and roll out each half, on a lightly floured surface, to an 7-inch round. Place on wax paper on baking sheets and bake for about 40 minutes, or until crisp. If the shortcakes are browning too much, move them down to a lower shelf in the oven. Allow to cool.

3 Peel, core, and chop the apples into a bowl with the lemon juice. Transfer to a pan, add sugar to taste, then cook for about 2–3 minutes, until just softening. Mash the apple with the mint and leave to cool.

4 Whip the cream or crème fraîche with the vanilla extract. Put one shortcake base on a serving plate. Spread half of the apple then half of the cream or crème fraîche on top. Place the second shortcake on top, then spread over the remaining apple and cream, swirling the top layer of cream gently. Decorate with mint sprigs and a few whole hazelnuts, then serve at once.